C000049661

Happy Birthday Gillian :) !
Something a wee bit different,
by my old friend, Gerry
Cambridge! Love, Dad x,xx
17/12/20

THE LIGHT ACKNOWLEDGERS

& Other Poems

THE LIGHT ACKNOWLEDGERS

& Other Poems

Gerry Cambridge *Gerry Cambridge*

Ayrshire
14.12.2020.

HAPPENSTANCE

BY THE SAME AUTHOR:

The Dark Horse: The Making of a Little Magazine, Happen*Stance*, 2016
Notes for Lighting a Fire, Happen*Stance*, 2012
Aves, Essence Press, 2007
Madame Fi Fi's Farewell and Other Poems, Luath Press, 2003
The Praise of Swans, Shoestring Press, 2000
'*Nothing But Heather!': Scottish Nature in Poems, Photographs and Prose*,
    Luath Press, 1999
The Shell House, Scottish Cultural Press, 1995
The Dark Gift and Other Poems, St Inans Press, 1994

ACKNOWLEDGEMENTS:

Thanks are due to editors of the following journals in which poems included
here have appeared, sometimes in earlier versions: *The Hudson Review, The
Café Review, Poetry Ireland Review;* and in the following anthologies: *Hunterian
Museum Poems; #UntitledTwo; Like Leaves in Autumn: Responses to the War
Poetry of Guiseppe Ungaretti.*

NOTE FOR VISUALLY IMPAIRED READERS:

The jacket colour is white and pale grey, with white occupying the top third. On
the front jacket the title largely fills the white section. Lettering is a thin sans-serif
cap. The words 'The' and 'Light' are biggest by far. Each starts on its own line, with
elongated verticals for both letter Ts and for the L in 'Light'. These verticals are
linked by colour (each thinly rainbow-striped with red and yellow brightest) and
by length (the L of 'Light' reaches up between the H and E of 'The'. Similarly the T of
'Light' stretches down between the G and E of 'Acknowledgers'. The rainbow effect is
also applied to the top and bottom horizontals of letter E in 'The', and to the central
bar H of 'Light'. The word 'Acknowledgers' is centred below in smaller, thinner caps
occupying the full width of the jacket. Below this, 'And other poems' is centred (very
small) with 'And' rendered as an ornate ampersand. The author's name is centred in
the grey area towards the foot of the jacket. The back jacket features descriptive text
about the author in a lowercase serif font. Below this an asterisk precedes a brief TLS
review quote. In the grey area, ten lines from 'Morning Thirty Years Later' (p. 17) is
printed in slightly larger black lowercase.

First published in 2019 by Happen*Stance* Press
21 Hatton Green, Glenrothes KY7 4SD
www.happenstancepress.com

ISBN: 978-1-910131-54-1

Printed and bound by Imprint Digital, Exeter
https://digital.imprint.co.uk
𝒴

CONTENTS

—I—

A BOX OF LIGHT

FROM A STOPPED TRAIN NEAR ARBROATH

Astonishing me now is how
those horizon clouds, the airy castellations,

such miles away,
framed by the carriage window,

are also with us here—
the original space travellers.

That boy could see them if he looked,
miniature cumuli

beamed across the world
and built again by photons with minute precision

on every attentive
or uninterested eye.

THE NATURE PHOTOGRAPHER

'The film emulsion for colour slides, Kodachrome,
was renowned among photographers for its brightness,
fine grain and vivid colours.'
> —*Dictionary of Film Photography*

Obsessional eighteen, I hunkered,
drenched by the tangling stems
millioned with wet crystal
skinkling into rainbow,
neck-cricked for the perfect angle,
with a Micro-nikkor bought
out of power-station hours,
to lock light-weighted gems
in the small bright rectangle.

I pity that young man
uncertain of his home,
nervy to rinse his mind
clean, to start again
in fantasies of order
glimpsed through the cramped pane
where the drops winked and flashed
and the spiders hubbed their lairs.
Life was Kodachrome.

THE FLOOD

Ordered rectangles of coloured light,
the storied kodachromes—what
were they but a plucking of shining drops
out of the constant flood and held
up to the gauging eye? I see them now
in their brilliant thousands stored
in the dark like small mementos
of a holiday in time before
the drench of rain and dazzle
in squally May
took everything unholdably on.
As it would, without end.

Make prints of them for the white walls
and the calm civil viewers
also seeking respite from that flood
in a dragonfly wing venation, or
the droplets held in this slung web,
an arrested glimpse through the pane
into a world of mathematic beauty,
as if that were the pinnacle and end
of all that sludge of dreck and blood,
exhibited here for praise
in gallery light of the gracious city.

THE LIGHT ACKNOWLEDGERS

—21st December

It's like a small
primary class of light,
this cleared room—
the lightmill on the mantelpiece, in its
tilted parallelogram
of blaze upon the wall
tinkling jauntily,
and the rainbow maker
against the pane
splitting the new rays
back to their spectra,
red, orange, yellow, lime,
blue and violet, more dazzling
than anything of winter Earth.

Whether the heart
breaks or heals, such
light acknowledgers
know what to do
with the gift
of unearthed clarity
even at this season:
the whirring device
of birling blades
and the glowing rainbow bits
rotating around the walls,
universal messengers,
the incandescent pollens
of our days.

ON DECLINING TO STAND AND STARE

Stepping out of the coffee shop
into St Vincent Street was sudden
late sun splashing daffodil
in exclamation, while black
mirrors of puddles serenely held,
upside down, white clouds in the blue
after the shower.

I looked back up the hill and saw
how the turning earth had swung the sun
into perfect alignment to pour
sure as a bullet's flight
down the length of the straight street.
In that fierce brightness the loud crowds, out
for their Friday Glasgow night,
the glamorous cloppers, the lovestruck couples,
the youths gobsmacked by cleavage—all
squinted and shone like a jeweller's window.

The word 'celestial' came
old-fashionedly to mind, as if
a door had been opened in a great hall
of brightness somewhere; till something closed the door
and I was glad. Whatever went on
in that lit space, its interests were not hours.

MINUS FIVE

—for Amit Majmudar

It took place in the night. Miles
up in the dark, out of untouchable height,
such a weight fell, such a vast whirl and chaos
       while the folk slept, snug as spoons
       in a drawer, under each heavy cover,
       dreaming in cossetted warmth
       of whatever. Then
it must have cleared, like a silent army going
tremendously away, leaving behind the wide
 star-pricked sky and the moon's
       liberated shining. So
       when I rose, blear-eyed,
dragged, reluctant, to the things of day
and the old wounds, and glanced out the door—
       a heartleap! Way
       into distance, all
 across the Highland morning,
the singular peaks, incandescent in the light
that had lifted itself out of amber to gold to the pristinest
       white in the eye.
And acknowledged only briefly—for already
 the kettle was clicking off at my back—
       summit on summit lit
     out under blue to forever:
     magnificent, and very cold.

A NEW WORLD

Soft and slow
the snow had made
with its calm tons
in the windless night
a white nowhere
of what was a road,
had folk unafraid
to wade among cars
backed up in miles
of huffing technology
extinguished as *Triceratops*
in the village street
when feet trumped wheels
for once. Shops
closed early, the usual
rules did not apply;
the globe had shrugged,
unburdened in millions
the weighted sky
on the thousands of roofs,
and the air was carnival,
the banked street live—
black blazers from school
edged with blue, shout-outs,
steam-breath, red cheeks, gangs
of rollicking laddies
pushing back-bumpers
of motionless cars
spinning their wheels.
O dazelight! O, young gaiety!

'THAT SCANTLIE FRAE THE CAULD I MICHT DEFEND'

—Ayrshire, 1988

Henrysoun, back in his century, has just
mendit the fire and beikit him aboot
but the flame in my gas fire had shrunk
to a peep. I laid the book aside. One a.m.,
December. The whole hilltop site was asleep bar me
in my box of aluminium in the frost-locked night.
I was starting to feel the chill. So
it meant carrying the just-boiled kettle out
under winter stars—*Hello Orion, Sirius, hello!*—
over crunching grass to the canister
of Propane at the kitchen window. I poured
the boiling liquid all down its skinkling red.
The metal crackled, as if I'd freed some demon; the gas
rushed through: a cloud of steam, lit by the window, rose
to that wide starlit air and thinned. And I crunched back
to the gas fire glowing the white grille red again,
opened the book like a door, and slipped inside. There
the enigmatic bard is telling his grievous story
in perfect Rime Royal. He will go on telling it
to the human end of time, the old grim tale
made beautiful. (My feet are warm again.
The fire hisses at the frosty dark.)
In that small box of light I still read him.

MORNING THIRTY YEARS LATER

Why should it choose this moment to arrive,
actual as then within my brain,
Arran's peaks so calm and pink in snow,
carmine on the eye, Himalayan in miniature,
in a winter dawn? And drew me out
frost-struck, unwashed,
sleep-creased, knowing it would go
in minutes, and somehow had to be
witnessed in its otherworldly quiet.

Bony as a fasted monk,
out of the unheated caravan
I am there again
in hastily thrown-on coat
and bare feet thrust in shock-cold shoes,
and blow into my hands
and stamp, watching the roseate light dilute
to the gleam of snowy amber,
the chill rime brushing my sockless ankles
as I return through the whitened blades.

WHOOPER SWANS AT WARWICKDALE

White oxygen of otherness. The dark road after showers
looped in a gleam up over the hill.
Wind-chimes stirred in the tall throats. There must have been
a dozen of them, lambent in that light, gliding across
the unrippled pool at the base
of the vertical sky, blown together by
my passing. Such graceful things:
but not to forget the antediluvian feet
dark as roof-slates, big as a man's hand,
webbed and flexing unseen under the surface.
I did not scatter them. My footsteps
started again on the moon-gleamed road.
A roof within a mile for me.
In the starry roof of their furled wings light years.

KINDNESS

   At Blair Estate
in the seventies,
  the wintered songbirds,
coal tits and robins,
  thrushes and finches, would
intrigue the walker, flit

  within inches, startle
with barb-bright nearness, their
  quick-eyed attention, even
alight to amaze on your palm
  for a moment
in the difficult season of glitter, due

  (so, at least, the rumour went)
to the slow old men in greatcoats, pockets
  packed with crumbs and seed,
up for air out of that other estate
  with their rooty hands
and thin crowns of snow.

CARDUELIS CARDUELIS IN MIDWINTER

They can still
alight, now and again,
on the wintery twigs
of my thought at this season
of the bleakening mornings,
the freezing dusks:

indomitable, vivid
twitterers, all
innocence before the Fall—
for little, it appears to me, could be
less to blame than such

unresting eaters of seed
imperilled in shadeless light
in their gold and scarlet,
their black and white.
So as I go

across the heavy day
I try to keep a space
for them, and sometimes think
I'd like to come back, if at all,
as one of their kind

in a troupe, a charm
of sinew and pinion and shine,
warming a little the mind
of some numbed one
in a future dark, as now
they do mine

CHRISTMAS EVE

I was crossing the footbridge over the Clyde
in the failing light near the last hour
for the shops in the city
when I was stopped by the siskins.
Eight, ten, thirteen, perhaps,
in the topmost twigs of an alder
at the height of my face, just feet away. Softly
they called to each other in the wordless calm,
intent on the seeds in the cones, and clinging
at various angles in their detailed greens:
quite unafraid of the passing stranger.

I had a train to catch but stayed and watched
for fully five minutes the dainty finches
busy and frantic to feed before nightfall.

Five minutes: out of time. Then, as one,
at some imperceptible gesture, they
flew off, undulating, as if all tied together
loosely in air, and settled, quite
invisibly, into another tree
down where the Clyde curved toward Glasgow
round the bend. I hurried to Central,
packed with its glitters and electronic boards,
its green tree full of lights,
the loaded Christmas shoppers,
the lovers' tiffs, the family fights,
the smartphones flashing their messages....
The whole loud city was a tinsel frenzy.
Back in their world, out in the dark miles,
the siskins, quiet now; the bare trees; the alder cones.

PRESENCE

Upstaged, at a poetry reading

I read the words aloud.
Behind me, from the bird hide
smelling of bare boards,
one evening of pink-staining cloud
the Loch of the Lowes

a tabletop of black
unrippled marble where,
in front of the watching dozen, straight
out of my right shoulder
the hen osprey flew off
her nest and flapped across,
with her inverted twin,
that whole width
of water. All
decorum cast aside

I too stood amazed
and followed the pointing fingers
when that peremptory bird
appeared to have decided
now was time to pluck,
like a brown trout out of the loch,
the world back from the word.

THE WAY TO SURPRISE A SPARROWHAWK

Ayrshire, 1973   —*For Steve Ely*

was to ascend, flaking the bark scales down,
the one Scots pine in the wood on a windy day
when the crowns clack-threshed and the sway
of the trunk through your clambering weight
was so mixed up with the air
galloping in off the Firth of Clyde
that, brooding up there on her old crow's nest,
and too well on for desertion, she
knew it only as the gusts you mimicked; when

your freckled face cleared
the rim of the twigs and, for a second—
the last shower gemming her scapulars—
her head swung round and your eye-pairs locked,
that instant was a stop to time and grief
till the feather-burst and the strident cries
took her, jinking, off among boughs and left you
alone with the mottled stupendous clutch
hot from her breast-blood, teetering high
in the creaks and chattering upperworld of leaf.

APPLE

In a granny smith my mother gave me yesterday, I noticed in my high
room after a few bites a brown worm-hole in the sizzling white flesh.
The worm would be long gone, surely. I kept munching and crisping—
and opened a jagged fissure on a grub's existence. I took the side
wall of his living room off—the whole universe, the clouds out in the
September Sunday morning, and the sun, could see him. I flooded his
darkness with vicious rays, and held the torn-open side of the green
globe up to my capillary-lightninged face. An encounter!

Grub and I gazed at each other. I touched his tiny brown mask with a
clumsy fingertip: he recoiled instantly, then began moving along the
opened track of what had been his secret burrow with small peristaltic
pulsations of his body—you could see, through the varnished white
integument, the cream mealiness of the apple flesh he'd eaten—to
where the track became a brown entrance and, beyond it, a tunnel.
By some obscure intelligence, he made for this, the surprisingly
elongating white body pulsating and shining until, like a train
disappearing, the whole length vanished into the sweet small house of
apple and the welcoming black.

So I suspended the half-eaten fruit by its stalk between finger and
thumb. And I was the god of this little world.

What dangles me with a like calm?

THE WORLD'S SMALLEST DINOSAUR FOOTPRINT

Hunterian Museum, Glasgow

One minute not in time
  before shop and love and word
the dainty dinosaur
  no bigger than a blackbird

left this single print
  immortalised in stone
like the foot of a miniature duck,
  the enigmatic, lone

insignia of its passing
  one hundred and seventy million years ago—
its great one-word poem
  it did not know

it left, chasing the end of life
  and did not care
in any case
  destined for mud and air

—II—

ON PAPA WESTRAY

ONCE ON AN ISLAND

—Papa Westray, 1987

We were in sunlight but the sea-haar
was a tall grey wall out there approaching.
The jersey I wore was the colour of mustard.
We were a ship, sailing into new weather.
First, long wisps across the fields:
in minutes I stood in an altered world.
The single track road dissolved at either end.
A tractor coughing gutturals somewhere
became Tommy of Maybo in his flat cap, leaning
onto his steering wheel
in the cooling engine's ticking calm.
Huge hands; the fingers muscled.
When I looked down, I saw my jersey
had gathered in hundreds the droplets,
pinprick spheres, minute clear worlds
that the haar had left in its swabbing passing.

I did not then as I do now
imagine the whole small vessel, its
minutiae of fescue and head of clover
and cranefly clung to the curve of a stem,
hung with its endless detail, becalmed,
till the ship sailed out
into the wide blue afternoon
and the billioned watery intricacy,
sunk in grey, evaporated
in the one expiating light.

BUYING GROCERIES ON A WINDY DAY ON PAPA WESTRAY

At seven that morning I woke in the croft on the island to gales
blowing the cloud-wisps over the face of the sun and away,
testing the crofts that were clinging minutely to earth here like limpets,
making cloud-shadows flee off over cow-dotted pastures; and later
walked to a speck down the long road. I swore that the gale was attempting
to gust me forever off, tumbling head over heels, up into space
to sun and the travelling clouds. Why should it not, for hadn't I often
said I had wanted that meeting with absolute things? I had said so—
easily! No one it seemed was about at that hour on the island,
Marie-Celeste-like its silence; not even east, down in the channel,
where miniature fishing boats, red, in the cobalt and white-flecked

                              bay bobbed
under the sharpening beams. That's till I noticed John Henry Rendall's
wife, as she hurried indoors from a washing, waving in distance
at the foot of the sky and leaving her linen so frantic behind. Oh,
never have I been delighted as much by mere flapping of washing,
distant and infinitesimal whites and bright reds and deep purples,
even though loving the sight of Atlantic beyond to shipped skylines:
crossing the meadow through buttercup crowds that were

                             manically lashing,
back to the croft where it stood on the hill with paint flaking its saltwood door,
never so glad of the carrier bags that were weighting my fingers
till under the tall sky I vanished inside to an undisturbed room

                             and a stone floor.

OLD CROFTER'S CARAVAN

Fifteen years of island winters
have left it like a bombsite,
the curtains tatters
and the windows
out. There's
where I would sit. He
would be over there, exhorting me, his one
front tooth jutting on his lower lip,
to 'tell thee trooth!' about him.

The pile of webby papers
above the spidered sink
had a letter from his mother
I wanted to take away
at least as one who cared
about what happened here. But
I read it and slipped it back,
beside where the blackie'd built
its stout and strawy nest
jigsawed now with shell,
to let the island weathers
scatter all, level each upright—
and it was a kind of joy that this
dross of seventy years
would all be swept
back to blue above that turquoise bay,
wind and rain, the travelling light.

BACHELOR CROFTER

The evening Tom Mackay came up
to where the croft stood on the hill
the showers were horizontal, blown,
though the world between stood dripping and still;
though he came through a shower and came
into the croft in boots and hat
like some piece of those weathers condensed
to flesh and difficult blood; and sat
with drops out of the sudden sky
dark-spotting the croft's stone floor.

He twirled thumbs, apparition; smelt
of dung and hay and sweat-reeked cloth,
and shuffled, so we thought he felt
awkward, though the place was his,
and us but visitors a while.
We lit the lamp, brought whisky out;
and soon a mingled snarl and smile
grew in his face, his squall-stung cheeks
red as a sunrise or sunset
when he leaned forward into light
as if away from the outside's wet
and, loud with trammelled love,
loomed his shadow up the wall.

I thought of the island silence
out there, its desertion, all
the sound the hidden sea's
distant stadium-roar beyond the hill,
and blood sun that went down there
as if cheered in its descent, until
it vanished from sight entirely—
as Tom. His tractor roared across the meadow,

turned north, switching tiny headlights on
that still were bright enough to show
ahead, frail gold grasses on the verge;
was gone. Nothing could be heard or seen
but uproar, and dusk's gleam-gashed sky,
where Tom Mackay had been.

—III—

IN GLASGOW CENTRAL

EASTER SATURDAY NIGHT
IN GLASGOW CENTRAL STATION

i

Here in the evening air of spring,
under the great glass roof
I sit at the coffee shop window,
my laptop open
like a book or a door,
distracted by the constant stream
of faces and bodies from right to left
and from left to right—
revellers, travellers,
all with their mysterious
purpose and end and unknown beginnings,
none of them, it seems,
noticing me, this middle-aged man
quiet on an April evening
while the song thrushes sit up country
on clutches of eggs matched by the blue
of a girl's dress as she passes
holding a book from Penguin Classics
(Aristotle? Plato?)
though I cannot see which one.

ii

Of course, the world burns. Regardless
the endless folk still move through this point
of departures, arrivals, meetings
under the clock: years,
the faces of children,
a brief sea in the eye,
yet hopeful tonight with the whole
summer ahead. O city of festival,
built on the dead!

iii

Where have you all come from?
Each of you here with your life, like mine,
the hugest thing, to you, and also
a mote, a grain of Saharan sand. All
risen up out of unknown beds,
bloodshot-eyed, washing the night off,
and passing before my astonished gaze?
I feel affection for you and your animal selves,
the weight of the body that, like mine,
has to be fed, kept clean, maintained,
so many
spruce and dapper and glammed up
with a force like the sun of Easter
opening its door of flame.

iv

No one is touched with grief this night,
so you would think in Glasgow Central,
where two young men, one either side,
half-drag their staggering friend,
his jeans slipped down below his pelvic bones,
boxer shorts on show. A half hour later
they pass again in the other direction,
the drunk one not too drunk for shame
yanking his breeks up at the back
in his aided hirpling with concerned, exploratory hand.

v

It's the grand tableau of a film in which
none of us knows the plot....
Here come the good-time girls, unabashed and joyful,
lipglossed, perfumed, fake-eyelashed,
out on the evening randan, six, eight,
magnificent horse-broad bottoms
in clingfilm skirts, dimpled thighs
ready to be clamped round a lover's neck or back—
all released from the cares of the week
to the winking gantry and deodorant-reeking men.

vi

And who is he, the older man,
strands of black slicked wetly back across his crown,
moustache of salt and pepper, his tweed and pristine
jacket of seasonal green
threaded with fine vermilion?
Dapper. What are his thoughts as he steps
nimble as a redshank through
the lively station with a glance
at me perched at the window
in a high, unaccustomed chair?
Who is observing whom?

vii

With the gift of youth they sweep like a twister
in their pink and white and yellow
through the parting stream of folk each way—
mini-skirt, cleavage, all bare arms and legs, stiletto heels
clicking along the marble flags. I think
of new-born foals,
impossibly long-limbed, but carnal;
or of the elevated, awkward grace
of giraffes progressing across a plain.
What does it feel to be like them, the gaze
of the lust-struck tracking you
as wood anemones follow
the sun across the star-concealing blue?

viii

A youth walks by with an eight-foot, green, inflated
crocodile under his arm. A thickly made-up lady,
elephantine calves wobbling at every step,
has on a lead a dog
so small it could fit in a sandwich.
Its little legs twinkle optimistically
holding its body three inches above the marble floor.
It goes in a head-darting fever of stimuli overload
in the great jungle of riotous giants—
like the daytrippers fresh
from hours in the sun, off the Ayr train—
a ragbag cavalcade, toddlers, youngsters, sun-livid mothers,
food-babied fathers, multiply-angled buckets and spades
in yellow and green and red trooping off into the evening—
an army returning out of the wars of light.

ix

A man is cycling, illicitly, slowly,
down through the milling station,
his lugubrious bulldog-cross in gray
(a row of teats asway on her underbelly)
looped on a lead strung from his wrist.
She suddenly halts and sits, almost
cowping him over the handlebars.
For seconds they gaze at each other in silence:
the dog, droop-eyed and jowled,
unrepentant, Churchillian, decidedly
not to be budged.
                    Stand-off.
The man—a vein-browed whippet—
unclips the lead from the bulldog's collar
and cycles on. The dog, insouciant,
continues to sit like a stone
in the constant stream, till after a decent interval
she stands and nonchalantly
wanders a couple of yards. Has her owner really
gone off and left her? A station official,
passing, clocks the unattended stray,
bends with a greeting, or an enquiry;
the tail stump
disconsolately wags. He mouths
at his walkie-talkie, and the dog
follows him a yard or two, then stops,
follows him a yard or two
then stops, down to where, I can see now,
her 'owner' stands beside his bike.
A lacklustre reuniting. A miniature tiff
in the swirling epic.

X

So often I have sat here watching,
part of the tale and out of it, as Whitman says,
seeing a name flash up with happiness
on the phone on the table, text messages
whizzing each second in thousands
across this city like arrows
unerringly hitting their targets.
The station stays. The people pass
and leave their stories. Thirty years back
one frosted winter night on the flagstones'
stained grey concrete, I stuffed a £10 note
in a fit of young-man grief
down the front of the greatcoat
of an old tramp stood like a bony horse
with the breath puffing out of his nostrils
and walked on, to my train. Now
a girl in a red jacket and a white top
hurries by on her way
into the infinities of evening.
There are wisps of fire all around the sky
silent above the city like some enormous gesture.
Out she steps, lightly into her past.

—IV—

THE VISITOR

THE VISITOR

Naw, Jim ud no be bothert if he came
Back here an fun ye in ma livin room— *found*
Ye ken he ayeways ses ye're his best freen. *says; friend*
Aye, an ah ken why he caws ye that, acaus *calls; because*
Ye nivver contradict im, yer too saft.
There's anely wan man is aye welcome
At this door, he ayeways ses: yersel.
Sit doon, sit doon, daen't act in such a rush!
He micht be back in meenits an besides
Yer drookit as it is; tek aff yer coat. *drenched; take off*
Listen tae thae gales and rain oot there!
Ye think the wather's cheyngin? Aye, me tae. *weather's changing*
It's cheyngin jist like Jim is. Daint lea jist yet, *don't leave*
Dry aff, he'll mebbe be in shortly! Aye,
Oot tae paint the toon bricht rid as yaeshal. *bright red as usual*
Turn this doon; ah anely keep it on fer company.

Ah'm no jokin, Davie, ye've jist nae idea
Whit Jim is like tae live wi as a man.
When we first cam thegither years ago *together*
It wus aw hunky-dory, ken, but noo—
Ah'm no shair whit has happened. Mebbe since
Aboot the time the wee yin went he's jist *little one*
Gone crackers awthegither. He'll jist sit
Oors at a time in front ae thon damn thing *hours*
Wi a face like fizz on im, an nivver sey
Wan wurd. Ah'll anely staun sae much ae that *only put up with*
An then ah end up geen im aw ah've left *giving him all I've left*
Efter the messages, an oot he jants. *for the groceries; gallivants*
Ah've nae time fer they fellas that he goes wi—
Ye want tae see them, Davie; mak ye shivver.
Ah've nivver asked im naethin; 's up tae him.
Aw o the wurld's jist wasted noo, he ses.
Mebbe that's richt enough, but still
It disnae mean ye should jist waste it faster!

Thon scrapheap o a motorbike he bocht—   *bought*
The highest pooerd thing that he could fin—   *powered*
It wus ma money peyd fer that, saved up
Bi aw ma bliddy cleanin in the auld folks' hame
Amang they geriatrics, ken, an look
He's still nae happier. His childhood? Aye,
Ah s'pose that's hud a haun, but loadsa folks   *had a hand in it*
Unhappy when they're weans. Ah've nae idea!   *children*
Ah ken his mither wus a hoor. Ah ses   *mother; whore*
Wan nicht, in here—he'd hud a drink—ah ses,
'Hit me if you want, Jim, but ah reckon
Fae aw you've ses aboot her that yer mither
Wus a hoor.' An he stared an stared an stared—
It made the hairs staun up aw doon ma neck—
But didnae lift a finger. She wus raised
Quite strict in a religion, ken; when she got oot
She jist cheynged awthegither. Is that richt!
Sae Jim'll mebbe end up saintly yet!
Ah widnae haud ma braith if ah were you.   *hold my breath*
Aften enough he'll come in here an greet   *cry*
An ah'll sey, 'Listen, Jim, ah don't ken why
Yer sittin bubblin there like that, she's no
Worth greetin fer.' Mebbe it's better though
Tae hae im greetin than the oappasit;
Ye didnae ken? Aye, he's gid at hidin things.
Yer gettin a different side ae things the nicht.
Yaeshally when ye come ah kin sey naethin   *usually*
Wi Jim there gabbin, twinty tae the dizzen,   *yapping*
As if he wus aw feart tae lea ye space   *frightened to leave*
Tae get behin his wa wi awkward questions.   *wall*
Aye. Ah mind a coupla years ago
A fella up the road geed me a lift
An in the caur he ses, 'Ah've got ten inches, hen,   *car; darling*
In case yer interestet'; 'Oh', ah ses,
'Ah've nivver hud a notion fer wee men.'
But like an eediot, when ah comes in   *idiot*
Did ah no open ma big trap, an tell
Ma wurser hauf the story; did he no   *my worse(er) half*

Stomp oot an up tae that lad's hoose an dragged
Him oot there in the street an geed im wan
Helluva doin so ah heard; sit doon!   *hell of a beating*
He micht be in at ony meenit noo.   *any minute now*
Ye canny go oot a nicht like that, until
It's slackened aff a bit. Wait on a while.
Jim's mebbe staggerin doon thon street the noo,
Er else he'll bang the door at fower the morrer   *four tomorrow*
Mornin; ah'll hae tae open up an let im in.
He lost his key a year ago, an since
We've no got roond tae hevvin im cut a new yin.
Ah don't ken why he's jealous noo at aw;
There's naethin noo atween us. Aye, ah ses
Tae sum ae they young lassies that ah wurk wi
'Ah think ah'll hae tae hae some wild affair,
Sumthin on the side'. Jokin, ken! Y'd think
In certain weys ah jist disgustet Jim,
The wey things hae turned oot. It wisnae that
They times ah hud tae hide fae im, an aw
His snuffin aboot me like thon Dobermann
He kept oot in the back shed fer protection;
Daft mutt got oot wan nicht an roamed the scheme.
They'd nae idea whae shot it—sae they said.

See men—ah cannae unnerstaun them.
Last week there in the auld folks' hame
Ah ses tae wan auld fella fer a laugh,
'Ye mustae been wan fer the lassies
As a younger man.' Here, bi Christ, did he
No chase me through the ward, ah hud tae hide
Inside the weemun's toilets till a nurse
Took im awa. Naw, he wisnae chasin me fer that,
He chased me ootae anger! Y'd ae thocht
He went that rid, he wid explode, or sumthin.

Oor Davie widnae hae turned oot like that.   *wouldn't have*
Eichteen he wid ae been this year; eichteen.   *eighteen*
That's him up there noo smilin on the mantelpiece.

He'd fancied sum new pairt, y'ken, fer thon
Auld bike o his, an hud been oan at me.
Ah mind he took some honey on a piece   *bread slice*
An' chowin it, an staunin oot the back
He stapped a meenit, turned an ses, 'Hey, Mam,
''ll ah get that fer Christmas?' An ah ses,
'Ah'll think aboot it Davie, if ye don't
Get intae bother.' Aye, ah mind thon simmer evenin,
Wi' lotsae weans playin aboot the scheme.
A roastin simmer evenin wi the sun,
An Arran fae ma kitchen windae here
Bonny wi the bricht clouds aboot its tops.   *bright clouds*
An that wus him, he went, then aw that happened.

When ah fell pregnant wi' oor Hugh ah hud
A dream aboot oor Davie. Ah wus at the door
Shoutin oot at him tae turn his heid
But he jist kept on goin, an he got
Wee-er an wee-er aw the time, as he ran aff   *smaller and smaller*
Across the fields, wee-er an wee-er an wee-er,
An didnae ivver turn. Jist whaur's he gone tae?
Sumtimes when ah try tae think ae it,
It fankles up ma brain, ah mean, wan meenit   *confuses my brain*
He wus here, an next, he wusnae. Thon thing,
Thon thing up in the Royal wusnae him!
Thon thing below the heidstane, thon's no him.
Sae whaur's he gone? Naewhaur? An whit
Dis naewhaur mean? Ah cannae unnerstaun it.
Ah've thocht aboot it time an time again
An' hoo, hud ah done sumthin else, like mebbe
Geed im his tea a different time, even sey
Five meenits either wey, it aw micht no hae happened.
Nane o it wid hae wurked oot hoo it did.
Nicht efter nicht ah've layed awake, an tried
Thinkin ae the reason we wus pit
Here in the first place, thinkin ae aw they
That lived wey back richt tae the stert ae time,   *the start of time*
An jist whit pynt there wus in aw ae it.   *point*

Ah coodnae see whit pynt there wus in it.
Ah'd like tae think the wee yin noo is dancin   *little one*
Forivver in sum big hivven, ken,
But sumhoo ah jist cannae.

              Yer jaickit?
Ye cannae go oot the nicht jist yet—hear thon
Rattlin at the windae: ye'd be lost!
'Mon, hae a cup ae tea noo an a sanwitch.   *Come on*
Och, he'll mebbe no be back the nicht at aw.
The anely thing tae come inside 'll be that nicht
Oot there, ah reckon, by the soond ae it.

—V—

DEPARTURES

SPIRIT

You are with me late at night
when I take the Sunday train
from Blantyre for the city. Premonitory
September, and the dark.
You look through my eyes out
of the near-deserted carriage
with its drunk and slumped subdued
rattling through each station—
Newton and Cambuslang,
Rutherglen and Bridgeton—
into the big lit space of Central
at Sunday 10 p.m., its after-party calm. And are
with me, companionable, warm,
all the way to my trudged-to destination
and the room of lipsticked kisses. How quietly
I leave you out in the night city. When
I step back into the tin-bleak light
in the motorway roar of morning, I have
to take your hand immediately again.

THE FIRST RING

It was the first ring, lost.
Your voice panicking
on the mobile in the vast
flatland afternoon—clouds, horizons,
behind the words.

I just looked down and it was gone!
The whole café searched for it!
Oh sweetheart, you don't think
it's an omen?
                    I bought another one,
a better fit, and calmed you with
A ring is only a symbol.

Three weeks, and the little ghost impression
is fading from my wedding finger.
What, that day, was inconceivable
has happened, and the body, at least,
replenishes itself—a migratory bird
leaving the mind's nest to gales and hail.

CROSSING THE FOOTBRIDGE OVER
THE CLYDE AT DUSK

The baffle-roar of the spate over the weir down in the valley
behind me, magnifies the silence of those high magenta clouds
tinied by distance on the skyline
with the otherworldly gleam in them at evening.

Far whoops of teenagers, small and particular, off
in the twilight at Blantyre. Wide-skied, dewy chill of autumn.
A first planet, white.
                              Our life together is over.

WATERSTONES CAFÉ, SAUCHIEHALL STREET

Can I take anything away?
asks the slender waitress
with her loaded tray; and wryly
I think, but do not say:
as if what I'd have taken
could quickly be lifted up
straightforwardly as an emptied cup
and washed back to white shining
for the next in line, down
for respite in this basement,
ice-browed by sub-zero air
pinnacling to a moon up there.

THE OBSERVER'S BOOK OF BIRDS' EGGS

Finding again
this little book
   at Moniack
after decades,
   too far removed to beg

   that you come back to me,
I could almost weep for when
   all worldly happiness was centred
on a redpoll's
   or a linnet's egg.

DISTANCE

Minus twelve at noon. At Uddingston Station
train after train cancelled, the plane
long flown if indeed it flew, nothing
to do but turn for home. How tenuous
the bright thread stretching
between you and me, and what
wide-opened faith I put in it, duffled and angsting
against the colossal weight of weather
there on the freezing platform,
my small breaths lost in the wide sky.

THE LETTERS

There remains the problem of the letters
and the cards. Hundreds of them,
sometimes three a day at first,
sent so freely, imagining a live future
or a present, bits of committed spirit
given up to hope. Especially
at the end, decisions all then taken, me
unaware and still professing uselessly
like a man on a headland conjuring ships
on an empty sea; under which
the great schools travelled on their ancient routes.

THE KEY

I threw the key at last
over the wall into the wood
one drab December night
of scunnerment
on my trudge home,
imagining its turning fall
as if in cinematic slow-
and-glittering motion,
to bounce among leaf-litter
and spiders scattering.

After its years on my
keyring, with its
twin and sharp-cut prongs
of iron, that world-revealer
left to rust, and not of any
risk or value now
in the multiplicitous world
hundreds of miles away
from its red door
and lock it would
not marry anymore.

THE SPARROWS OF BOTHWELL

already have a sense of spring,
chirruping at the bathroom window where
   every May they nest within the wall.
Although it is grim January,
   and they are small,
their irrepressible notes today
      chip away
like miniature axe-strokes
at the great grown tree of dark
   which shelters me.

HERACLITEAN

'No man ever steps into the same river twice,
for it's not the same river and he's not the same man.'
            —*Heraclitus*

Morning in the city takes us onward.
We speed away from each other for ever.
I love this musicked coffee shop at Central
at eight a.m., or nine, its workaday
laptops, books, and the caffeine tang
and the dipped biscotti that carries me
out of the pull of you and the downdrag grief.
Morning slantlight angles in and sets
each table and cup and spoon in its
exclamatory dazzle. The whole city
rouses and stirs like a giant beast,
car windows will be flashing on the distant motorway
under the high white clouds,
the airport bus will be crammed with new arrivals
speeding to the centre
from Newark, Madrid, Sumburgh, Dubai.
A man rolls up his newspaper and steps
into the current that will not end.
Morning takes us onward. *You. I.*

—VI—

DESTINATIONS

AN OLD STORY

After a long absence
my uncle arrived
one night across the sea
from Ireland. Some terrible thing
had happened. Frost had streaked
his sideburns with furious care,
strand by strand.
I had not seen him for a year.
Although a child, I knew
a wintrier air
had laid its hand on him.
I stared as he ate supper.

Here on the Ayr train,
travelling to the old woman
my mother has become,
who served that supper to him,
something about the way
my hands rest on my knee
under its threadbare corduroy
brings this memory back. Tonight
I am that man of all those years ago
stepping in out of the dark
across the sea.

REQUIEM

First anniversary: 17.08.2011

The thin priest maundered on,
mumbling into the microphone,
telling the jaded stories, told
a thousand times before, explaining
them to his small and, one would suppose,
ignorant congregation. It seemed no more
than a stagey amateur bit of theatre
with the tinkle of the bells and the white
and purple robes. And suddenly
swallows were going crazy above
the tall blue-lit cupola overhead, so loud
they drowned out the old man's words
with rushes of chirrups and riffs
distracting the listeners. You

took it for a sign from the dead man who,
in his last days on his spotless hospital bed,
had raised his head to the swallows flickering
out over the Ayrshire fields, then let it fall.

I took it for a sign of earth, those unignorable notes
with all the excitement of Africa
in the flexing bloodrust gorgets at their throats.

IN GORDON STREET

Something about—
                    in these
new dark nights of cold,
the clocks gone back and me
duffled and happed—
passing in Gordon Street
the entrance to Central
and through its arches
that glimpse of orange names and times
lit in their neat columns on
the electronic boards—
Crossmyloof, Euston,
Birmingham New Street, Ayr—

touches me
                    as if
my father looking through my eyes or that
part of me that feels him there
exclaimed, astonished, still
covetous in his bony grave

for I could board tonight
to any of those unearthly destinations
whatever train I chose

RELATIONS

Your scowl was the nest of a long-tailed tit
Your sitting in front of the TV through the hours of a frosty night
   was the querulous waver of a tawny owl at Annick
Your weeping bafflement at the obdurate teenage silence escaping over the fields
   was a panicky sister's arms around my stiffened neck
Your plugging the loupe into one eye socket for a wheeze-concentrated faff
   with wires and a radio crackle's resumption
    was a micro-nikkor and a dragonfly's ommatidia
Your wrapping an electric blanket's filaments round the outside pipes in winter
   was a kerned 'A' cap in Poliphilus
Your peering over my shoulder as I put together a sandwich in the kitchen
   was a skylark's nest with a hatching cuckoo
Your fall was a green jacket and a blue jacket for you and for your father
Your Son-of-Beelzebub mood-swings were the self-chilled adolescent ablaze
   in my forty-eighth year
Your plucked-chicken wash at the kitchen sink in socks and sagging y-fronts
   were the powerful muscles of my calves
Your slowing breaths were the terrible descending numerals showing
   the blood's oxygen, going
The capillaries miraculously fading in your face in the minutes after was
   the hushed greying of the sunset sky
The blood specks on your fingertips from the pinprick samples were the small
   constellations on a wren's egg
My hands rinsed under the tap are yours
My spasming cough is your last days
My going away is your going away in the country of my chest
But there is nowhere to go away to now
You are becoming me, felt with a look or a way of turning my head
The chromosomes on their constant quest I am the advance scout for
The memorial voyage I have thwarted
Whose coffin I will be.

LAST RITES

That my father was always turned out trig
with a red tie and a white shirt
and a matching buttoned jersey
the blue of a starling egg
and brown brogues polished to shining, was all
down to the pride of my mother.

She carefully chose the clothes for his corpse
and when at the Co-op funeral parlour
I insisted the lid be taken
completely off his coffin, she was right in there
immediately, with a single-minded animal intent,
ensuring they had changed the socks
on her darling of fifty years ago.

WISH

Billy Blaney, his snottery and blubbery
buck-toothed smiling face,
the twin snailtracks of mucus from his nostrils,
appears to me now in a kind
of childhood shining, his ingratiating way—
N-n-now w-what d'ye m-m-make
o' that then, G-g-g-ger'd?—treating me
with the deference I must have taken at
that simian age for my due.

All of us mocked him constantly
for each tremendous effort he put in
to climb the fence of every tripping consonant
into the green field we occupied so thoughtlessly,
not seeing what had happened him

as now I think I do. At a wedding years ago
I blurted my apologies, to his
pretended, I believe, non-remembering.

Billy Blaney, I apologise the most,
half a century too late,
for my self-serving wish to be forgiven. There
is the green field
now. Here, every fence
that's waiting to be climbed.

THE ANNALS

Margaret McLaughlin is dead
at eighty, my mother tells me—
Poor soul, at rest, after long ailment, who
four decades back in her tight sweater's pure-
white-as-a-cushie's-egg
was imagined joys,
wry and knowing, in the nightly fumblings
of acned boys now frown-ploughed men

And Dougie her man, renowned then
to Malcolm Boyd of Barnahill
for the unprecedented height
of each load of swaying bales he could bring
singlehanded in from the fields, is lost
in his head down some unknown road
he won't return from now

And Douglas their son—
an only child the mother spoiled,
whose look was hers—
died before them both;
he found a curloo's nest before I did
and, from somewhere, got
a swan's big egg in pastel green;
we singled neeps together
for Davy Smith of Middleton
(both farm and him gone too)

I write them down in my black notebook
punctiliously, in annals that no one
else will keep, through a day of smirr   *fine rain*
on a calm hillside, particulars that gleam
like the clear beads weighing
down the frail heads
of the June wildflowers

A SECRET SAFE TO SHARE

Outside the *Starbucks* on Buchanan Street
in the swelter of this Good Friday,
in the first of the three small limes
(barely a sapling, really)
a goldfinch pair have built
their dainty nest on a branch
(if it could be called a branch
so like a twig it is)
a dozen feet up in the tracery
decked with the new and flimsy leaves.

Over the Gucci bags, the perilous stillettos,
the cool dudes in their shades,
the pushed prams, the mini-skirted bottoms,
the skinny calves of the teenage boys,
the guitar and voice of the busker
singing lost love's despair

is the little masterpiece, so delicately made,
moss and lichen-patched, lined with hair
snatched by eager beaks from wherever
and worked well in up there,
a cradle now for the four, or five, or six
embryo-darkened eggs.

Quite unfazed to share
the swarming street of commerce, the plucky finches
ovening to life the dotted shells
I coveted as a boy! Who pass in age,
and notice so precariously in air
beak and tail just visible—
at which I glance, and smile, and move along,
with a sharp, wild flare of joy.

A BIRTH

for C & M

Dragonflies were hatching
at Sevenacres Mill
in the skanky pool
on old mine workings
on the thistly hill
in the June morning.

Anchored to stems
the coming sympetrums
drawn by light were giving
birth to themselves,
the larvae of glaur,
having crawled up
to the bending blue
of a new existence;

and recalling them there
I felt the thrill
of a further life
I could not have imagined
in the freshness of morning,
a calm revelation
in the wet nets of wing.

NOTES ON THE POEMS

'The Nature Photographer', p.10
Micro-nikkor: a 55mm f3.5 macro lens, specially designed by Nikon for close-ups on film down to 0.5 lifesize. *Skinkle*: to sparkle or glitter.

'The Light Acknowledgers', p.12
21st December: the winter solstice. *Lightmill*: this little device, invented by Sir William Crookes in 1873 and known also as a Crookes Radiometer, is a glass bulb with a partial vacuum inside, containing four black metal blades set on a spindle. Direct sunlight heats the blades, causing them to whirr around. *Rainbow maker*: another small light device, made up of a Svarovski crystal (acting as a prism) below a small solar panel. The device is usually attached to a window by a suction pad. Sunlight powers the solar panel and this turns a mechanism of cogs which turns the crystal; the latter splits the light into the colours of the spectrum, which slowly revolve, luminously around the room.

'On Declining to Stand and Stare', p.13
Like 'The Flood' on p.11, this poem was part of a commission for an event at Celtic Connections in January 2017 curated by musician and writer Liza Mulholland. The performance was themed around the concept of 'Standing and Staring', based on W. H. Davies' popular poem 'Leisure', which begins: 'What is this world if, full of care, / We have no time to stand and stare?'

'Minus Five', p.14
The dedicatee, Amit Majmudar, is a fine Indian-American poet, novelist and diagnostic radiographer with a particular interest in the classic, epic texts of world literature.

'That Scantlie Frae the Cauld I Micht Defend', p.16
The title means 'I could hardly keep myself warm from the cold'. It is drawn from Robert Henrysoun's medieval Scots poem 'The Testament of Cresseid', which Tom Scott in *The Penguin Book of Scottish Verse* called the greatest poem in Scottish literature. I first read it in the Ayrshire caravan I lived in for twenty years, 1977–1997. The italicised second line of my poem is a slight recension of Henrysoun's original. *Beikit me aboot*: made myself warm.

'Whooper Swans at Warwickdale', p.18
Whooper Swans, *Cygnus cygnus*, called after their high, 'whooping' cries, overwinter in the UK from Iceland.

'Kindness', p.19
'Blair Estate': the grounds of Blair Castle, formerly the ancestral home of the Blair family for more than 900 years. In the seventies it was owned by one of the last of them, Colonel Borwick, who allowed me and others access to the grounds for nature photography. A kindly man, he had lost both his sons in a tragic car accident. The poem's old men would have come from a housing estate in nearby Dalry.

'Carduelis Carduelis in Midwinter', p.20
Carduelis carduelis: goldfinch

'Christmas Eve', p.21
The *footbridge over the Clyde* connects the Lanarkshire village of Bothwell to Blantyre and its train station.

'The Way to Surprise a Sparrowhawk', p.23
Sparrowhawks often take over old crow's nests. The wood where it nested across the Annick Water near the caravan site on which I lived was known locally as 'the witchwood'.

'The World's Smallest Dinosaur Footprint', p.25
This poem was commissioned for *The Hunterian Museum Poems*, an anthology based on objects in Glasgow's famous museum, edited by Alan Riach in 2017.

'Once on an Island', p.29
I spent two summers on Papa Westray, one of the outlying islands of Orkney, in 1987 and 1988, and often visited at other times. I stayed in a waterless, unheated dwelling at the north of the island belonging to Tom Mackay ('Tommy of Maybo') who died in the autumn of 1997. He is the speaker in 'An Old Crofter Speaks' in my first collection, *The Shell House* (1995). He lived in a caravan surrounded by breeze blocks at Mayback, on the east shore of this small island.

'Easter Saturday Night in Glasgow Central Station', p. 37
Glasgow Central Station was opened on 1st August, 1879. In 2017–18, it

was the twelfth busiest station in the UK and the busiest in Scotland, with nearly 33 million passengers, and over 38 million people using the station. The concourse was originally grey concrete, but later refloored in stylish pale marble in the mid 1980s. In 2017 the station was allegedly more popular with its users than any other in Britain.

'In Glasgow Central iv', p. 40
hirpling: limping

'In Glasgow Central ix', p. 45
cowping: throwing, tipping

'The Visitor', p.49
This monologue can be thought of as a companion piece to 'An Old Crofter Speaks', mentioned in the note to 'Once on an Island'.

'Departures', pp.57–66
This sequence draws on a relationship that ended in 2014.

'Crossing the Footbridge Over the Clyde at Dusk', p.59
A first planet, white: this would be Venus.

'The Key', p.64
Scunnerment: completely fed up, with a hint of disgust.

'Requiem', p.70
My father, Brendan Joseph Cambridge, died on 17 August 2010. The chapel is St John Ogilvie's, Dreghorn, Ayrshire.

'Relations', p.72
ommatidia: facets making up the compound eye of a dragonfly. *A kerned 'A' cap in Poliphilus*: the serif typeface Poliphilus is notoriously idiosyncratic to typeset in its digital version.

'Last Rites', p. 73
trig: neat or smart, particularly in dress.

'A Birth, p.77
A small pond on old mine workings at Sevenacres Mill in Ayrshire hatched sympetrum dragonflies on summer mornings. *Glaur*: mud.

ABOUT THE AUTHOR

Gerry Cambridge founded the transatlantic magazine *The Dark Horse*, still Scotland's leading poetry journal, in 1995. He is also an essayist, print designer and typographer, with a background in natural history photography and a lifelong interest in the natural world. He lived in an Ayrshire caravan for twenty years before leaving to become a Brownsbank Fellow in Hugh MacDiarmid's former home for 1997–1999. He has been a Royal Literary Fund Writing Fellow at the University of Edinburgh (2006–2009) and at Glasgow Caledonian University (2010–2012). In his early twenties he was, as far as he knows, one of the youngest ever regular freelancers, specialising in nature articles, for the UK *Reader's Digest*, which at the time (the 1980s) had a monthly circulation of 1.5 million copies.